WELCOME TO CHINA

COUNTRIES OF THE WORLD

China

by Monika Davies

BLASTOFF! READERS 2

BELLWETHER MEDIA • MINNEAPOLIS, MN

Blastoff! Readers are carefully developed by literacy experts to build reading stamina and move students toward fluency by combining standards-based content with developmentally appropriate text.

Level 1 provides the most support through repetition of high-frequency words, light text, predictable sentence patterns, and strong visual support.

Level 2 offers early readers a bit more challenge through varied sentences, increased text load, and text-supportive special features.

Level 3 advances early-fluent readers toward fluency through increased text load, less reliance on photos, advancing concepts, longer sentences, and more complex special features.

★ **Blastoff! Universe**

Reading Level

Grade **K**

Grades **1–3**

Grade **4**

This edition first published in 2023 by Bellwether Media, Inc.

No part of this publication may be reproduced in whole or in part without written permission of the publisher. For information regarding permission, write to Bellwether Media, Inc., Attention: Permissions Department, 6012 Blue Circle Drive, Minnetonka, MN 55343.

Library of Congress Cataloging-in-Publication Data

Names: Davies, Monika, author.
Title: China / by Monika Davies.
Description: Minneapolis : Bellwether Media, [2023] | Series: Blastoff! Readers : Countries of the world | Includes bibliographical references and index. | Audience: Ages 5-8 | Audience: Grades 2-3 | Summary: "Relevant images match informative text in this introduction to China. Intended for students in kindergarten through third grade"– Provided by publisher.
Identifiers: LCCN 2022018172 (print) | LCCN 2022018173 (ebook) | ISBN 9781644877166 (library binding) | ISBN 9781648347627 (ebook)
Subjects: LCSH: China–Juvenile literature.
Classification: LCC DS706 .D385 2023 (print) | LCC DS706 (ebook) | DDC 951–dc23/eng/20220420
LC record available at https://lccn.loc.gov/2022018172
LC ebook record available at https://lccn.loc.gov/2022018173

Editor: Elizabeth Neuenfeldt   Designer: Gabriel Hilger

Printed in the United States of America, North Mankato, MN.

Table of **Contents**

All About China

Beijing

China is a big country in Asia.
Its capital is Beijing.

China has the world's biggest **population**! More than one billion people live there.

N W E S

Beijing, China

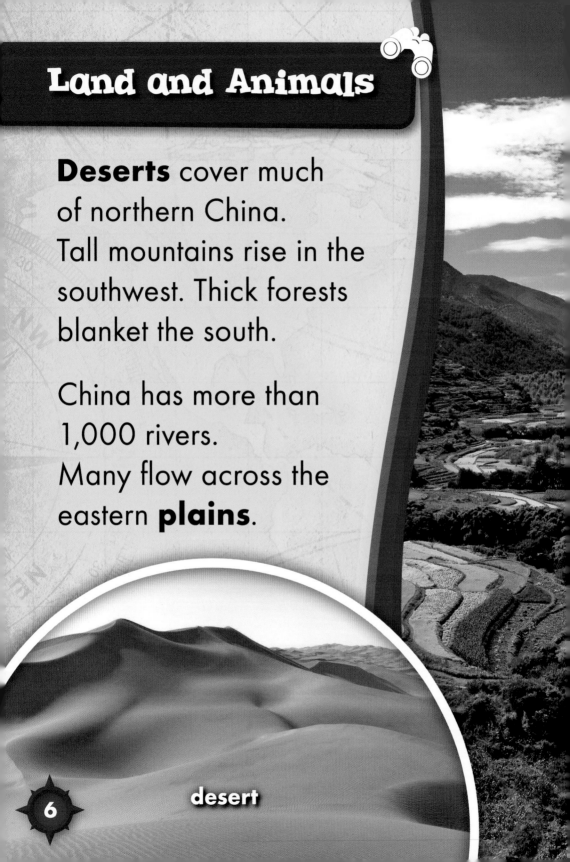

Deserts cover much of northern China. Tall mountains rise in the southwest. Thick forests blanket the south.

China has more than 1,000 rivers. Many flow across the eastern **plains**.

desert

Yangtze River

Size: 3,915 miles (6,300 kilometers) long

Famous For: third-longest river in the world

China has chilly winters.
Northern China is usually
colder than southern China.

Summers are warmer.
It rains a lot in the south.
Typhoons sometimes strike
the southeastern coast.

Many different animals live in China. Giant pandas chew on **bamboo** in mountain forests.

giant pandas

Animals of China

giant panda

snow leopard

wild yak

Chinese alligator

Snow leopards and wild yaks roam in the mountains. Chinese alligators swim in the Yangtze River.

Most Chinese people are Han. Others have different backgrounds. Many Chinese people speak Mandarin.

Most people live in the east. China's biggest cities are there.

Shanghai

12

table tennis

basketball

In China, basketball and soccer
are top sports. Table tennis is
also popular!

Many Chinese people practice **martial arts**. Tai chi is a favorite.

tai chi

Rice is a **staple** food in China. Many people eat rice every day.

Chinese Foods

rice

Peking duck

dumplings

Sichuan pork

making
dumplings

Peking duck is a famous dish.
People also enjoy dumplings.
Sichuan pork is another
common food.

China's Spring **Festival** honors the new **lunar** year. Families travel far and wide to **celebrate**.

Spring Festival

The Moon Festival is in the fall. Families eat mooncakes. China's holidays bring families together!

China Facts

Size:
3,705,407 square miles
(9,596,960 square kilometers)

Population:
1,410,539,758 (2022)

National Holiday:
National Day (October 1)

Main Language:
Mandarin Chinese

Capital City:
Beijing

Famous Face

Name: Yao Ming

Famous For: a professional basketball player

Religions

Buddhist: 18%

other: 8%

folk religion: 22%

none: 52%

Top Landmarks

Forbidden City

Great Wall
of China

Li River

Glossary

bamboo—a tall, tree-like grass that grows in warm regions

celebrate—to do something special or fun for a big event, occasion, or holiday

deserts—dry lands with few plants and little rainfall

festival—a time or event of celebration

lunar—related to the moon

martial arts—different sports or skills that first started as ways to fight or stay safe

plains—large areas of flat land

population—the total number of people who live in a certain place

staple—a widely used food or other item

typhoons—huge, powerful, and harmful storms that often happen in Southeast Asia

To Learn More

AT THE LIBRARY

Grack, Rachel. *Giant Pandas*. Minneapolis, Minn.: Bellwether Media, 2022.

Meinking, Mary. *Let's Look at China*. North Mankato, Minn.: Capstone Press, 2020.

Spanier, Kristine. *Great Wall of China*. Minneapolis, Minn.: Jump!, 2021.

ON THE WEB

FACTSURFER

Factsurfer.com gives you a safe, fun way to find more information.

1. Go to www.factsurfer.com.

2. Enter "China" into the search box and click 🔍.

3. Select your book cover to see a list of related content.

Index